LIGHT SHOW
Reflection and Absorption

Jack Torrence

The Rosen Publishing Group's
PowerKids Press™
New York

Published in 2009 by The Rosen Publishing Group, Inc.
29 East 21st Street, New York, NY 10010

Book Design: Daniel Hosek

Photo Credits: Cover © Stephen Strathdee/Shutterstock; p. 5 © Al Rublinetsky/Shutterstock; p. 6 (left) ©
Petros Tsonis/Shutterstock; p. 6 (right) © Svetlana Privezentseva/Shutterstock; p. 7 (left) © Losevsky Pavel/
Shutterstock; p. 7 (right) © Serg64/Shutterstock; p. 9 © Paul & Linda Ambrose/Taxi/Getty Images;
p. 10 © Elena Elisseeva/Shutterstock; p. 12 © Tadija/Shutterstock; p. 14 © Charles Gupton/Stone/Getty Images;
p. 17 © Supri Suharjoto/Shutterstock; p. 18 © Josef Szasz-Fabian/Shutterstock; p. 19 © Taxi/Getty Images;
p. 20 © Steve Dunwell/The Image Bank/Getty Images.

Library of Congress Cataloging-in-Publication Data

Torrence, Jack.
  Light show : reflection and absorption / Jack Torrence.
     p. cm. — (Real life readers)
  Includes index.
  ISBN: 978-1-4538-0096-0
  6-pack ISBN: 978-1-4358-0100-4
  Hardcover ISBN: 978-1-4358-2974-9 (library binding)
  1. Light—Juvenile literature. 2. Light absorption—Juvenile literature. 3. Reflection (Optics)—Juvenile
literature. I. Title.
  QC360.T67 2009
  535—dc22
                                        2008036790

Manufactured in the United States of America

CONTENTS

LIGHT IN OUR WORLD

When we look around our world, we see colors, shapes, people, buildings, and much more. Did you know that we aren't really seeing "things" when we use our eyes? We are actually seeing the light that **reflects** off the things and travels to our eyes.

Light is made up of all the colors you can think of. We see colors because all objects reflect some of the colors in light and **absorb** others. Grass, for example, absorbs all colors except the color green. Green light reflects off the grass and enters our eyes. This is why grass looks green. A ripe banana looks yellow because it reflects yellow light and absorbs all other colors. Black objects absorb all colors. White objects reflect all colors.

On a sunny spring day, Central Park in New York City is a very colorful place.

All light comes from a **source**. Our main source of light is the sun. During the day, the sun lights our world and allows us to see everything in it. The sun even allows us to see the moon. The moon has no light of its own. We see it only when the sun's light hits it and is reflected.

Light begins at its source and travels out in all directions in straight lines until it hits something that blocks it, absorbs it, or changes its direction. We've all seen our shadows on a sunny day. Have you ever thought about what causes your shadow? Your body blocks the sun's light. The dark area you see on the

Fire and lightbulbs are also sources of light.
Can you think of other light sources?

ground—your shadow—is caused by the blocked light.

Sunshine makes us hot on a summer day because we absorb the heat and light of the sun's rays. When sunlight reflects off a puddle, it changes direction and hits our eyes. Can you think of other ways light is blocked, absorbed, or reflected?

WHAT IS LIGHT?

Light is a form of energy. Energy is the power to work or act. Other forms of energy include heat and electricity. Much of the light that hits an object turns into heat when it is absorbed. Also, heat can create light, as it does when we burn wood for a campfire.

Light is the fastest thing in the **universe**. The sun is about 93 million miles (150 million km) from Earth, but its light only takes about 8 minutes to reach Earth! The light from the sun that doesn't hit Earth travels out into space. It won't stop until it hits something. Stars in the night sky are many **billions** of miles away from Earth. It takes billions of years for light from the stars to reach us. This means that we're seeing what the stars looked like billions of years ago. Some of these stars may no longer exist!

The moon looks different to us depending on the positions of the sun, Earth, and moon. Sometimes Earth blocks the sun's light and casts a shadow over the moon.

Many of the scientists who first studied light believed that it was made up of waves, like those formed when you throw a rock into a pool of water. Later, scientists believed light was a stream of very tiny pieces—or **particles**—of matter. They noticed that when light hits an object, the object stops the light from continuing. The result is a shadow. They also noticed that light reflects off objects, somewhat like the way a ball bounces off the floor.

Scientists today know that light can act like both waves and particles, although they aren't sure why. The scientific name for a light particle is "photon." Scientists also know that rays of light with waves of different lengths create different colors. The shortest waves make violet light. The longest waves make red light.

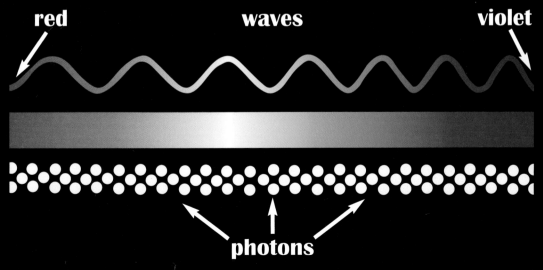

red   waves   violet

photons

REFLECTING LIGHT

What happens when light reflects off the surface of an object?
Picture an imaginary line **perpendicular** to the surface. Rays of
light striking the surface are called **incident** rays. The angle
between an incident ray's path and the imaginary perpendicular
line is called the angle of incidence. The angle between the
imaginary perpendicular line and the path of the reflected ray is

called the angle of reflection. The angle of incidence and the angle of reflection are equal.

Rays of light reflected from a smooth, shiny surface such as a **mirror** all go in the same direction. That's why you see your reflection in a mirror. However, most surfaces are uneven. Rays reflected from an uneven surface go in many different directions, and you don't see your reflection.

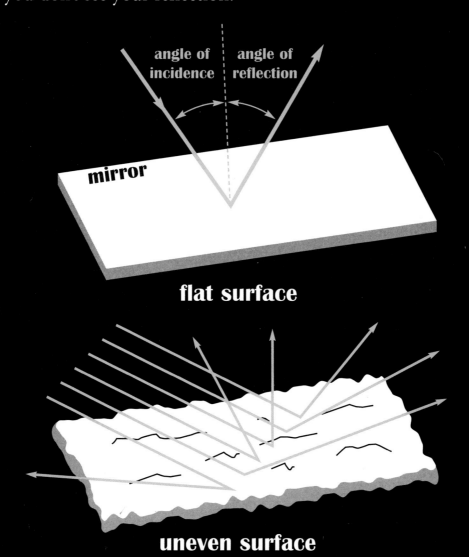

angle of incidence   angle of reflection

mirror

flat surface

uneven surface

Fun house mirrors have curved surfaces. Light reflects off of them in different directions, making our reflections look funny.

Because mirrors are such good reflectors, we use them for many purposes. You're likely most familiar with mirrors used in your home. We use them to see ourselves when we comb our hair and get dressed. Dentists use small mirrors to see inside a person's mouth. Many **microscopes** use small mirrors to reflect light onto the object being viewed. Mirrors of different shapes and sizes are also used by car makers, barbers, and artists, to name just a few.

Some mirrors are curved. Mirrors that are curved out make things look smaller than they actually are. Mirrors that curve in make things look bigger than they actually are. Depending on how close an object is to a mirror that curves in, the reflection may look upside down, too. Curved mirrors are used in some **telescopes**.

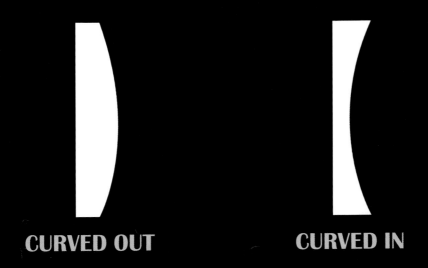

CURVED OUT   **CURVED IN**

ABSORBING LIGHT

All surfaces reflect at least some light. However, all surfaces absorb light, too. This means that some light energy passes into the object it hits instead of reflecting off it. Even a mirror absorbs a small part of the light that hits it. When this happens, the energy changes from light energy into heat energy. This is why we get warm when we lie in the sun.

Dark surfaces absorb more light than surfaces with light colors. A black surface reflects some light, but it absorbs much of the light that hits it. The energy from the light will make the black surface warm. You get warmer when you wear a black shirt on a sunny day than when you wear a white shirt.

It's better to wear a white shirt at the beach. You might get too hot in a black shirt.

BENDING LIGHT

When light travels through space, there's nothing to get in its way, so it travels in a straight line. Different **mediums**—such as air and glass—cause light to move faster or slower. When light reaches the place where two mediums meet, some of the light is reflected, and some of it is absorbed. Some of the light is also **refracted**, or "bent." This means that the direction in which light is traveling changes. This change of direction is caused by the change in the light's speed as it passes from one medium to the other.

Have you ever noticed that a straw in a glass of water looks broken? This is because light waves from the part of the straw in the water refract when they pass from water to air. The discovery of refraction led to the creation of the first lenses and telescopes.

A prism is a piece of glass with a special shape. When light hits a prism, the glass refracts it and splits it into the colors of a rainbow.

EXPERIMENTING WITH LIGHT

Scientists have been experimenting with light for many years. You can do your own experiment with light. You will need four mirrors, a table, and a friend.

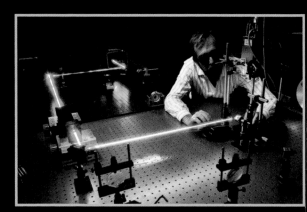

Place two mirrors near the edge on one side of the table, facing the middle. Place the other two mirrors on the opposite side, also facing the middle. Next, you and your friend kneel down across from each other on the remaining sides so your eyes are level with the surface of the table. Look into one of the mirrors. Move it until you can see another mirror. Keep moving mirrors until you can see your friend's face using all four mirrors. This experiment shows how light moves in a straight line even after reflecting off a mirror.

You can have fun by drawing or taping a drawing of eyes on one mirror, a nose on another mirror, ears on another mirror, and a silly mouth on the last mirror! Now how does your friend look?

LIGHT EXPERIMENT

STEP 1: Place the four mirrors along two opposite edges of the table, facing in.

STEP 2: You and your friend kneel down along the other two edges of the table with your chins resting on the table.

STEP 3: Move the first mirror until you can see another mirror in it.

STEP 4: Keep moving the mirrors until you can see your friend's face using all four mirrors.

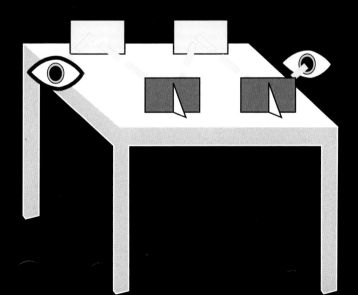

creates a shadow when blocked

form of energy

the sun is our main source

light can be reflected, absorbed, or refracted

allows us to see our world

LIGHT

an uneven surface reflects light in many directions

travels in a straight line

black absorbs more light than white

acts like both a wave and a stream of particles

can make heat and is sometimes created by heat

GLOSSARY

absorb (uhb-ZORB) To take in and hold on to something.

billion (BIHL-yuhn) One thousand millions (1,000,000,000).

incident (IHN-suh-duhnt) Striking a surface.

medium (MEE-dee-uhm) Matter through which something, such as light, passes.

microscope (MY-kruh-skohp) An instrument used to see very small things.

mirror (MIHR-uhr) A smooth, shiny surface that reflects an exact picture of something placed in front of it.

particle (PAHR-tih-kuhl) A very small piece of matter.

perpendicular (puhr-puhn-DIH-kyuh-luhr) Having to do with two lines that cross to form right, or 90°, angles.

reflect (rih-FLEKT) To throw back light, heat, or sound.

refract (rih-FRAKT) To change the direction of a light ray by making it move more slowly or more quickly.

source (SORS) The place from which something starts.

telescope (TEH-luh-skohp) An instrument used to make faraway objects appear closer and larger.

universe (YOO-nuh-vuhrs) Everything there is.

INDEX